How to Forgive

The Healing Power of Making Peace With Yourself

(Learn to Take Control of Your Life Through Forgiveness)

Clifton Maldonado

Published By **Andrew Zen**

Clifton Maldonado

How to Forgive: The Healing Power of Making Peace With Yourself (Learn to Take Control of Your Life Through Forgiveness)

ISBN   978-1-998038-69-5

No part of this guidebook shall be reproduced in any form without permission in writing from the publisher except in the case of brief quotations embodied in critical articles or reviews.

Legal & Disclaimer

The information contained in this book is not designed to replace or take the place of any form of medicine or professional medical advice. The information in this book has been provided for educational & entertainment purposes only.

The information contained in this book has been compiled from sources deemed reliable, and it is accurate to the best of the Author's knowledge; however, the Author cannot guarantee its accuracy and validity and cannot be held liable for any errors or omissions. Changes are periodically made to this book. You must consult your doctor or get professional medical advice before using any of the suggested remedies, techniques, or information in this book.

Table Of Contents

Chapter 1: Defining the Past

"To forgive is to set a prisoner free and discover that the prisoner was you."

-Lewis B. Smedes

The first step towards healing an injury from the history is to identify the root of the issue the exact circumstances, and the way it made you feel. Recalling painful memories could be difficult as the aim isn't to go back and relive the events that occurred. It is important to view it as what it was an event that occurred. The hurtful area from your own inner view for some time It's now time to look at the situation from a different perspective.

The process of defining your past can help to begin your journey towards forgiveness for yourself. Instead of allowing the events to determine your life and the way you feel it is your turn to determine what you'll do in the future. That means you do not need to believe that you're trapped in the feelings of the incident. Now is the time to change the way you think as well as your memory. You won't be able to remember the events that occurred and it'll make you aware that you're only a single person who has made an important decision that is now time to make a change.

Our minds record historical events in many ways. There is the memories of events, images of what we perceive through our minds' eyes as well as the feelings we experienced. The sum of all these make up the reality we're currently experiencing. If you are suffering from suffering or illness, a lot of instances, it's due to not being able to resolve our feelings. It is commonplace to place the burden of our past onto ourselves and carry it along with us like a dress we've never wanted to remove. Now is the time to get rid away those outdated views let go of that burden and find a fresh way.

Method: Find a calm location to lay or sit down. Get rid of all distractions and sounds. Relax for three minutes and shut your eyes. Visualize yourself in front of a film screen. Imagine yourself moving around in a zigzag pattern, moving from place to location. Remember the triggering incident. What's important is to view it from a different perspective, similar to an account being presented. Being an outsider in this situation, try to describe what occurred to you.

When you read this tale in a different perspective Take note of the things that are different than the way you were thinking about it prior to. Do you notice something distinctive in the person you're viewing? Does this person seem angry? Overwhelmed? Did you know that there were events that lead to the present circumstance?

Make sure you are as objective as possible regarding what transpired, but without engaging in emotional reactions. Be aware that you're an observer from an outside view. When you observe what happens be aware of how you're being. Are you feeling sad to this person? Are you feeling empathy or empathy for what the person went through? Is this situation any different than the way you had been considering it prior to this?

You should take as long necessary to process the situation. After you're done then slowly return to your present. Breathe deeply and then sit back.

Then, pull off a journal or notebook to write down your feelings. Be honest about your feelings, however, don't let yourself fall down a spiral. Note down everything you witnessed as well as what you thought about that person whom you observed. When you're done go through the notes you have written down. There ought to be obvious differences between the way you recalled the event prior to this activity and the way you perceive it today. What do you think are the different? What do you have been saying to yourself about the events that occurred?

This exercise is to help you recognize how much you've been telling your self. The exercise isn't meant to condone every action, but rather discovering a different approach to get through the feelings and emotions that surround the events you experienced. When you have a clearer view could you realize how difficult you've put in your own mind? Do you have a brand new consciousness about the events that occurred?

Recognize your emotions.

The first method can let you know that you might be looking at your circumstances with a bias. This can be helpful to know so you can begin to understand the emotions you feel and figure out what they are. There is no way to alter your feelings until you begin to comprehend the impact of your feelings and how they are connected to the current situation.

Sometimes, the best way to get through a tough time is to be able to feel the feelings of the experience. Being able to feel your emotions isn't necessarily an issue. It could, in reality it can be extremely healing. If you decide to confront the issues you are experiencing, make sure to complete the process in order to work. What I am referring to is that you must experience the pain of hurtful previous events, so you are able to move on. Perhaps you're thinking, I'm not going to experience those emotions, but they are hurtful! This is why it's vital.

The body and brain are required to deal with events, specifically traumatizing or painful ones. The bad memories are likely to hold greater influence on our memory than positive ones due to the fact that their power of the energy was more powerful and intense. Allowing your body and brain to experience these emotions as they are felt, then process them and decide to get over them significantly more effective than trying to get over the issue. The spiritual writer Eckhart Tolle said "There is a equilibrium between honouring your past while not getting caught up within the past. It is possible to recognize and grow from your mistakes before moving to the next step. That's what it's known as forgiving yourself."

Method: Sit in a quiet place and breathe deeply. Think about the incident which upset you. Then, focus your feelings. It's important to determine the emotions. Are you feeling anger? Frustration? Overwhelm? Let yourself be aware of the sensation. Let it flow through your body, and then exit from to the side on your head. It's now completely felt and let go of that feeling. If you ever consider that scenario it will be a different experience. The energy that comes from the emotion won't be as potent in the event that there's any energy left. Consider your emotions as energy. The idea is to allow that energy to flow throughout you rather than causing it to get stuck in the body, where it will do damage to you.

Are you obliged to someone for an apology?

Next, you must be aware of the individuals who were involved in the incident. Do you have a history of hurting anyone else? Do you have more than one? How will that affect the process of forgiveness? If another party was at fault with the situation, you might find it essential to talk with this person to acknowledge their thoughts regarding what transpired.

If you believe you are owed somebody an apology, you must take the initiative to work to a point where you're able to make that happen. When you're ready meet with the person, and let them know you'd like to chat. It might be beneficial to make an appointment at a place that is public like the park instead of using the phone to talk. When you're there it is not necessary to get into the details. Just keep it brief concise, short and clear. A lot of times, people will not be able to remember the things you do. Accept any criticism and then apologize for it with sincerity. Once you have acknowledged the feedback, your job is complete. It's up to the individual (or individuals) to decide whether they'll accept your apology. After you've made the apology for yourself and you have made it clear, the rest is of your concern. The person who accepts it can choose to do so or decline, but it doesn't matter to you. You've done your part. It's not enough.

No longer are you the victim.

A second important step you be required to do when it comes to forgiveness yourself is to change your character instead of being a victim and being fully responsible for what has occurred. If you are a victim, it means that you've refused to accept the responsibility for what happened to yourself. The way you view life is the result of something happening to you' rather than thinking that you are the cause of your circumstances'. This can be an unsteady slope that only leaves you and the people in your life feeling hurt. Stop being the victim of any circumstance. You have the power to decide your life. Don't let victims the power to control your life. A decorated veteran of the military and motivational Speaker Steve Maraboli has his thoughts on the notion of being a victim "Today is a brand new day. Don't allow your past to hinder your path to success! Today is the day that you are no longer the victim of your circumstance and begin to take action toward living the life you desire. You are in control and have time to design your future. Be free of the notion of victimhood and discover the reality of your potential. Your destiny was not for the mundane existence!"

Don't put off finding your happiness and peace.

Learning forgiveness is for you to achieve peace. It can also help people find joy as well as prosperity and satisfaction. The thing that most people don't know that these don't come from 'finding They're something developed through your experience. However, that doesn't mean you shouldn't incorporate them into your daily life now. Some people think they'll "be content at some point ..." they're happy or "be better as time goes on. ...". This mindset can lead to disappointment and unhappiness. Do not think of your accomplishment as something that can only take place in the near future. Let it happen now. Simply talking to yourself and using phrases like "I am at peace," or searching for little items that bring you joy and carrying out those activities are the first steps to creating healing feelings in your everyday life.

Take a look to the future.

Finding ways to be at peace with yourself, and then taking a positive step towards new goals can help to let go of the old. Release your hold on your past by looking at the future ahead. It can help you design the life you desire. Your life is the outcome you create for it.

After you've gone through the practice that helped to define the events you experienced and have a new viewpoint on the events now is the time to go on to the next step of your quest: eliminating any guilt or blame out of your life.

Chapter 2: Guilt and Blame, the Toxic Duo

"Release the desire to replay the same negative experience repeatedly within your head. Do not become an adolescent of the past, by constantly reliving and replaying your errors. You shouldn't be reliving the things you could have done differently. Let it go and release."

-Les Brown

Guilt is a loop which is hard to get away from. It is a path that doesn't allow you to leave since you continue to loop back to where you made the blunders. As you repeat the same cycle, you start to blame you for having let it take place in the first instance that again triggers thoughts of guilt. That's where the trap lies: the blame and guilt.

If we speak of guilt and the infinite circle that it places us in, we're discussing a feeling which can become limiting, and sometimes even fatal. It can trigger a range of feelings that can include shame, anger, and even frustration. When it gets severe the guilt could turn into a debilitating condition. Furthermore, guilt can do little to rectify what the mistake you made. It just fuels an emotional burning.

How to get rid of guilt from Your Life

The Percy Jackson book series, the author Rick Riordan adequately describes the anxiety Percy feels within The Lightening Thief: "All I could think about was that teachers might have discovered the illicit collection of candy that I was selling in my dorm room. Maybe they'd realised that I downloaded my Essay about Tom Sawyer from the Internet but never actually read the novel, and then they'd take my mark. Perhaps, even more importantly, they'd have me take the time to read the entire book."

While this story is a bit humorous, it's an accurate depiction of how the brain operates. Percy experiences guilt over his actions, and makes up a list of undesirable outcomes that could result as a result of his actions. The same happens to us. The actions we take can trigger thoughts of remorse, and even unwelcome results. The thoughts and emotions build as time passes until guilt is able to make it's way into every crevice of our lives.

Do not be hard on yourself.

Whatever the cause of your error, judgement or a bad choice which led to less than ideal results You must be aware that the mistake you made to get there, and you're the reason. It could be that you did as best you could at the time.

Perhaps you had to deal in unresolved anger, or another feeling that led you to the decision. Perhaps you've been disoriented and, in the context of it was the way you believed you ought to have when you did. It doesn't mean that you're wrong, but it's a sign that you didn't intend to commit a wrong which could have hurt you or other. To forgive yourself, you must realize that there is no superpower in you. According to the saying, you're just a human being.

Tell us your experiences.

A lot of people feel it is necessary to express their feelings in a person who can aid them to understand the reasons why something occurred and the reason for why specific steps were taken. Sometimes, it is difficult to discern these feelings on your own therefore it's crucial to locate a friend whom you can confide with. It isn't the intention of anyone to provide a miraculous answer to self-imposed guilt. But, a trustworthy person, such as a friend or family member that is a great listener will help you clear the clutter inside your head and help you see things from a new viewpoint.

There's no reason to have more.

The most ineffective way of thinking is to think "I ought to have done that." ...""". This is similar to an illusion made of the illusion of smoke and reflections. It is possible to say that"could have," or "should have" done whatever however, when you get to the end day, the statement will turn into a lie. If you are responsible for your actions There isn't a notion of a "should. The only thing that matters is the fact that it isn't. Avoid falling into the trap of blaming your self with words like "I should have." ..." that." That's experiencing regret, sadness and wondering what could be.

It's crucial to think of things in a different way when you think about it. If you realize that you frequently blaming yourself for mistakes with words like "I ought to have done this," ...", attempt to alter the phrase to "That occurred. I'm not going to make the same mistake the next time. What could I do differently this time?"

Learn something from your experiences.

The world is full of learning events, and every moment offers a lesson. Learning from an unfavorable situation might initially be difficult. It's been a while since you've worked to shift your view regarding the issue. It's now time to alter the situation once more, and figure out the lessons you're required to know.

There are two things that are certain in life taxation and death. Include "We all make mistakes" to the list of those two because it's one of the absolutes. When you begin to look for the lessons that an experience can teach you, you'll begin looking at it as what it really is as a valuable learning opportunity.

Today, you know more than you did in the past.

It is said that "Hindsight is 20/20." If you could know how you acted back and you were to do it again, things will have changed, wouldn't they? You didn't. It's unfair to feel guilt for a thing that, had it occurred today and you had the chance to do something differently. Let yourself be the way you once were and be who you currently are. Every stage of your life is special and significant.

Certain things are beyond our control.

It is our belief that we have control over all we encounter. However, if you take the time to consider it, a large portion of the events that life throws upon us is not within our reach. As an example, suppose that you missed an appointment at work because you were forced to stay at home with your child. The boss might be tempted to make you feel guilty about having missed the deadline, but what alternative did you choose? It was your parent instinct to ensure that your child received the highest quality treatment. Don't be hard on yourself over life's events that you are not in control over. Be aware that life is unpredictable and you are getting through the process.

Consider yourself to be unconstrained by guilt.

Spend some time imagining that you're completely free of worries about guilt.

They are no longer yours. It is possible to move around your life in a simple and considered manner. Be aware of the peace and tranquility associated with your fresh identity. These feelings are totally achievable. The difference is huge in the moment you put your mind and imagination to make what you desire for your life.

After you've completed some effort to rid yourself of that guilt you've felt It's time to get rid of another harmful emotional state from your life that is blame.

How to Stop Blaming Yourself

The act of assigning blame to an act or series of actions. It is possible to believe that a circumstance was beyond our hands, or that others were involved who coerced us into doing something that we weren't comfortable with. In any case the situation, we assign the blame in order to assist our brains cope the way things went.

There is a tendency to blame someone else in certain circumstances. What is harm to blame someone for their errors? It just fuels an ember of negative and harmful feelings that could, eventually get out of control. The same happens as when we blame ourselves and our own mistakes. These steps will aid you in stopping blame-making yourself and, in turn get rid of the negative energy.

Make it yours.

It's not synonymous with taking accountability and owning an issue. When you commit a blunder and accept the blame and want to fix the mistake in whatever way you can. Making yourself blameworthy, however is an attitude of victimization, in which it is impossible to rectify your situation. Think about the distinction between the two options. Do you blame you for the situation? Are you taking on the blame? The entrepreneur Robert Ringer said, "Everything changes for the better when you take ownership of your own problems."

Find ways to cultivate self-love.

People who continually accuse themselves of their mistakes do not love themselves. Self-love is an essential attribute that helps you overcome guilt. Self-loved people are not blaming self-pity for the mistakes they have made. They acknowledge that they are working on their own. Try to identify the one thing you admire every single day. If it's not easy just tell yourself that you're doing well. Building self-esteem is one of the elements that allow you to be able to love. Love yourself doesn't mean being a jerk but rather accepting someone that is distinctive and amazing regardless of the fact that you've made several wrongs on the way.

Meditation is an excellent approach to build the self-esteem and confidence. Spend some time every morning to let your mind be free of any thoughts. When you're in a calm, peaceful environment take a deep breath, shut your eyes and take a few deep breaths before saying positive thoughts, like, "I will learn from my mistakes and move on" and "I am loved, and I am good enough". Allow your brain to guide your thoughts to the words it desires to be told. The exercise takes only about a minute and can be highly effective.

Do not be too negative.

It's impossible to love yourself when you're constantly blaming yourself for every small thing you say or perform. The people who criticize their own and other people are hiding deeply negative emotions. The act of pointing out the flaws of others is not going to aid in letting go of self-blaming. Instead, focus on catching yourself if you are beginning to judge. Refrain from the thoughts and redirect the focus to something positive. If you find this challenging, make an effort to be quiet. Like Bambi famously put it, "If you can't say something nice, don't say nothin' at all."

Create realistic expectations.

Continuously striving for perfection every single thing that you do is not just unattainable, but it could result in mental damage. Accept that certain circumstances in your life may hinder you from reaching perfectionism. This is true for the relationships you have with people, managing your finances as well as developing your professional abilities. Each of us has limits and weaknesses that we are all unique to ourselves. It's possible to conquer them one step by step. If you're looking to ascend an uphill, you must to start from the beginning. Let yourself take a break, and let the rest of your life flow. You can continue to keep putting one foot before the other.

Make yourself available for what you want.

If you are finding it hard to let go of blame, perhaps it's time to get some old-fashioned R&R. How long did you last took care of yourself? Consider "What would make me feel better right now?" Setting aside time and taking time to do specific things can surely aid in reducing the burden of blame. Take a massage or for a walk in the woods, go on the time to take a relaxing bubble bath... The possibilities are limitless.

Be compassionate...

...to yourself. It's difficult to be blaming yourself constantly often. It is possible that you have learned to the importance of blame from authoritative people in your life, for example, parents or siblings. There is a chance that you've been accused of doing things throughout your life. Consequently, you learnt to accept make excuses from an early stage. When you got older and grew older, blame was a constant sensation in your daily life. When you believe you have the capacity to communicate with your inner child who lacked confidence to question the negativity of others. Let the child know that he or has a special place in the world, and no one is to take the blame.

Give yourself a hug as well as understanding and affection.

Moving Forward Without Guilt and Blame

The removal of guilt and shame from your life will surely, transform the way you feel about yourself. It will make you feel more content, and be more inclined to take positive steps as well as be able to handle your emotional issues effectively. According to the Dalai Lama profoundly said, "We can never obtain peace in the outer world until we make peace with ourselves."

In the chapter that's at the conclusion of the book Alternative Techniques for Forgiveness and Healing, you'll discover more ways to handle negative emotions and thoughts. Alongside the information described in this chapter make use of this guide to alleviate your thoughts of blame and guilt.

In the following chapter in the next chapter, we'll look at the impact these changes are having on how you view the world in the future. It will be like looking at the world with new eyes.

Chapter 3: Seeing Life Through New Eyes

"When you forgive, you in no way change the past - but you sure do change the future."

-Bernard Meltzer

French writer Marcel Proust uttered one of his most memorable quotes regarding the evolution of a different viewpoint: "The real voyage of discovery consists not in seeking new landscapes, but in having new eyes."

You should now have a better understanding of your own life in a different way from the way you saw it at the time you began this book. Understanding that everyone makes mistakes and useful lessons to be learned from these mistakes is a change in perception that will help recover from your mistakes. This approach helps you shed the burden of guilt and blame, and takes away negative emotions with a fresh perspective of what you can expect to happen for you in the future.

If you're wearing glasses you know what it's that it is like to look at things with new eyes. This results in a 180-degree shift in your perception of every aspect of your life. The adjustments you've created and are continuing to create are equivalent to having a brand new pair of glasses. The way you see things will continue to be in a different way from now on.

It's not over yet but. Still, there are important adjustments which need to be made. Here are some mind-centered strategies that will assist you with your journey to forgive yourself. They are and then some tips to keep your body in good shape.

Pay attention to your thought processes.

Set yourself the challenge of taking all day to keep track of your thinking. What is it that you are thinking about your thoughts the most? Do your thoughts tend to be either positive or negatively oriented? Do you engage in heated debates about yourself if events don't go according to plan? If you're planning to alter your perspective on an incident in the past and to accept the blame, you need begin changing the way in which you process your thoughts, all the time. The goal is to make your circumstances, not create the situation worse. This is why you need to alter the negative mental patterns that cause people to think of things negatively. Reversing negative thinking habits will enable you to create a space where forgiveness does not just exist but flourish.

Abraham-Hicks's pivoting method:

The number one New York Times best-selling book, Ask and it is Given, written by Esther And Jerry Hicks, gives a effective method known as Pivoting. It can help you change unwelcome thoughts into ones that are sought-after. The book says: "...whenever you feel negative emotions, and this helps you realize you're focusing on things that aren't yours, you'll take a moment and think, "I have a list of things I don't need, but what am I thinking about that I really want?"

This easy but effective method can help break down the force of negative thoughts. Simply asking a question and focusing your mind on the things you want to change your attitude and gives you an entirely new perspective. The practice over time can help change your thinking habits towards a positive outlook.

Break your news addiction.

In the meantime you may want to stay clear of the news media and other social media. It is due to the fact that majority of stories that are reported in media have a negative shock factor. The kind of news story that is told will draw readers in with anger and horror. If you are trying towards a new way of thinking and to forgive, it's easy to stay away from the kind of stories. Instead, be surrounded by positive experiences. There's an abundance of books, CD's, and applications that are designed to inspire and motivate.

Serve others by living a life.

Apart from positive literature and programs being active and helping those who is in need will lift you up by countless ways. Giving the time to aid an individual or cause that gives you emotion that's incredible. When you're able to step away from your thoughts and assist someone poor, sick, or struggling it opens up the door to love to yourself as well as other people. A wise person I have known told me, "To love is to serve."

Steer away from negative effects.

As well as limiting your exposure to negative news, it is also important to take it a step higher and stay away from negativists or people who make you feel negative. It is possible for negativity to be being absorbed into you which is why it's crucial to stay away from the negative influence. It's very hard to change your behavior with people who are negative. You must find a method to get your life away of people who affect your life in destructive ways.

Be like a kid.

Have you ever thought about how kind children can be? They may be injured in one moment and smile one minute and smiling the next. It is because they are able to let the hurt pass. They don't tend to hold any grudge or hostility towards anybody. An embrace and an "I'm sorry" will quickly help a child forgive. Even though we're grown ups does not mean that we shouldn't carry an attitude that is similar to a child. Make time to rekindle your inner child and let that child emerge.

Make an image of yourself.

Famous writer Neville Goddard talks about the significance of creating a picture within your head of how you would like things to happen. If you'd like to be in peace and the point where you're able to accept yourself as you are, spend some time to imagine this picture in your mind. You can even imagine the way you feel when you reach this point. What kind of clothes would you choose? What do you think of? What scents do you get? Create it as vivid as realistic and true as you possibly can. Imagine the life you could live If you were completely in equilibrium with yourself, and work on becoming that kind of person. When you are able to practice the person you wish to be today it will be a magnet for the things you want to your life. Things you desire start to appear in your life with greater ease. Neville adds that the subconscious mind isn't aware of what is the difference between something which was actually occurring as opposed to the picture it holds in your mind. This means that you might just be creating what you would like to achieve. Make sure you don't delay becoming the person you'd like to be and do not allow procrastination take away your ambitions. Do what you'd like to be right now regardless of whether it's only in your mind.

Big-picture Perspective.

If you find yourself in a situation that is too difficult It can be beneficial to look back, and take a look at the larger view. This helps you see the issue you're faced might seem overwhelming or insignificant, but if you consider it from the perspective of a bird's-eye view it becomes smaller and more clear which allows you to observe things you could not be able to see prior. Sometimes, broadening your view of your problem can aid in finding solutions that to problems you never knew existed.

Actionable Tips for Keeping Your Body Healthy

Take time to be outside.

Nature can be one of the most potent remedies for easing our suffering. In the outdoors it is a chance to engage all five senses, allowing us to slow our brain's activity and increase mental clarity. Outdoor exercise physical activity may positively impact the mental health of our brain and can help to reduce stress and anxiety. If you go for a quick walk through a park, or climb a mountains, spending time among nature, flowers and trees is a great way to relax your mind and body.

Readers are Leaders

The phrase that entices millions of children throughout the world to get books is relevant also for adults. There's something in losing yourself in a tale or discovering something you're interested in that makes you look at things in a different way (more important things). Select a book genre that is interesting to you. As you say, get lost to a story and then come back on the other end of it having a fresh view.

Give technology a break.

There's no need to get rid of your laptop to throw in the garbage bin; but technological advancement certainly has its role in our world. But, taking an escape from technology as well as using the World Wide Web can help to provide much-needed relaxation. There are times when connecting with a variety of people, and having so much to be doing can lead to a serious feeling of overwhelm. Try small adjustments like making a trip to the store or going for to a walk rather than surfing the internet. Keep your smartphone to the side for a part of your working day even if you don't have to. Instead of sticking the earbuds on, you can listen to the sound of nature. Shut off your TV at night, and curl up with your favorite book. This will calm your mind as well as ease stress.

Find a passion.

One of the advantages by having a pastime is that it forces you to take your time and explore your abilities. Are you not sure if you possess many talents? What do you like to do? Are you a gardener? Are you a music lover and are looking the art of playing an instrument? How about picking up a painting canvas outside and then sitting down painting a gorgeous scene? Are you a collector of items? It's a vast array of options when it comes to finding something you enjoy to work on. Choose a hobby or a skill that you'd like getting better in, and then go after it!

Laughter really is the best cure.

As with exercise, laughter can have the potential to enhance your immunity, ease tension and enhance your mood. Begin with a pal and look for things to be laughing about. Participate in a funny play or a stand-up comedy show or even watch a hilarious film. The act of smiling releases endorphins into the brain that act as a natural pain reliever.

Get some nutritious food.

Healthy eating is more beneficial for your body than maintaining a slim figure. Foods are energy sources as every other thing else. A meal of food that isn't healthy may sound as if it's a good idea but the effects last for a long time. If you're looking to become an individual who is happy and energetic, it is essential to eat healthy food and drink that's energetic. Healthy food choices boost the creation of beneficial chemical substances in your body. It helps to regulate hormones as well as blood sugar levels and even mood. This makes the process of forgiveness appear much easier.

If you implement these techniques, you could feel much more relaxed on both sides. Changes to your thoughts as well as your body can make you live a more fulfilling life and be greater in meaning. You've been through plenty! The time has come to discover what every experience has to teach you. You can always discover in any situation. In the following chapter we'll examine the lesson you've learned from your own experiences.

Chapter 4: Finding the Lesson

"Without the rain, the flowers can't bloom. If you don't face challenges, neither will you."

-John Di Lemme

Each experience offers us the possibility to draw something useful from it. We are the ones to learn what we learned from our difficulties. The lessons we've learned are how to look at things from a different angle. It's important to do this because it is when we look at things in a different way, we let the lessons to bring us the greatest growth. According to a well-known quotation by Eric Bates goes, "There are no negatives in life, only challenges to overcome that will make you stronger."

The majority of the time whenever we are confronted with a difficult circumstance, we will are spending a significant amount of our time fighting the situation. It's not something we want to have in our lives, and so we aren't willing to take it on which is why we build an enormous amount of resistance to the issue. Refusing to fight something just doesn't make a difference to the issue and can even create an environment that we do not wish to see, due to our fixation on the things that aren't functioning. If you've heard the expression, "What you focus on expands" and it's clear how destructive combating a problem can be.

There are two options when confronted with a challenge. You can choose to fight and make walls of negative thoughts while we look at the situation as a normal part experience in life. Although you may not want to go through the same thing that you've experienced, acknowledging the reality of what happened grants you control over the circumstances. By resolving what's occurred, rather than getting stuck in the mess and avoiding it.

Consider "What have I learned from this experience?"

Based on neuroscience research, whenever you have a query, the brain works to discover an answer. If you ask yourself thoughtful questions regarding what transpired can provide the possibility of a new perspective. Instead of viewing what's been done as something that you be regretting, why not allow yourself an opportunity to see something positive in the situation? The challenge will aid you in understanding what you're made of and how much you are able to take on, and what would like to achieve in your the world. A great book which talks about the importance of answering questions and the potential that they hold. The book is called What If Everything goes Right? Written by Mendhi Audlin. She describes why your brain thinks the way it does when you ask a question and what it does to alter your life.

Consider, "What could I have done differently?"

It is a good idea to consider what might be the outcome if you taken different decisions. In some cases, seeing the way you might have taken an alternative decision on things can assist you in making various choices for the remainder the rest of your existence. When you come back, you'll understand more about it, and will approach the situation differently.

Consider, "How can I help other people through what I've learned?"

The measure of your character is when you apply the lessons you've gained from adversity to assist other people. The people who give advice are those who've been through hardships and gained the knowledge to live their lives better due to their experiences. Being someone that people be inspired by for example, a coach, counselor, teacher or even a close friend, could provide meaning in your life, and also assist in healing.

Never give up.

This story provides an excellent illustration of how one can be able to forgive themselves regardless of the obstacles.

A man whose name was Bill lived the majority of his 20s in an Wisconsin prison, for various offenses. The prisoner was offered the drugs from a young stage of his life, and eventually began to become incredibly addicted. They drew him into a world full of dreams and excitement. The alternate reality he experienced was intriguing and returned time and time.

All of it came to a halt following an evening of drinking with a friend from college. The two parted ways after which the party-goer went home, and fell asleep. On the following day, Bill was arrested for giving the friend drugs. The friend was arrested and charged. to 10 years of prison without the possibility of early release.

In shock, he initially thought of every way to escape, even suicide. In the end it became clear that he didn't intend to live. He slowly accepted the realities of his new lifestyle. He began to understand the consequences of his choices caused him to be in this situation. The man also realized that how the remainder of his existence was be governed by him, and what he would agree to do in the future. He was forced to make difficult decisions regarding his future. He figured he would be accountable for the results of his error.

He decided to read books and do research so that to make the most sensible choices that could place him in a better place to achieve. He studied the famous leaders throughout history and how they thought and acted and how they behaved. The idea was that, if he desired to succeed when he was released from prison, he'd have follow the same path as someone who was successful, as well as make a variety of different choices.

A few days ago, one of prisoners offered Bill an opportunity to consume the drugs he had illegally smuggled into. In that instant the prisoner paused in confusion, unsure of what he should do. He went back to his cell to contemplate it and, after a moment, he realized that if he wanted remain free of drug abuse and corruption, when finally free, he'd need to begin immediately. He told the prisoner and did not look at him again.

Bill was released from prison aged 31 and had little money, no work or college degrees. Bill knew that he needed to work to achieve the level of success the way he wanted to, which is why he immediately went into work. He found a job that paid 10 dollars an hour then a year later, began his own company. In the following five years, the entrepreneur successful in selling over one million dollars worth of products. He made smart use of his money and invested it in index funds as well as real estate. He was married, and kept building his portfolio of financial assets.

The blog he writes on, Wealth Well Done tells the lessons he has learned while going through this difficult phase of his life. The author says "Beyond a physical prison, the biggest prison you can put yourself in is negativity inside your mind."

Bill was at a point in which he might have lost hope in his own. He made mistakes he was not pleased with and paid the price of the mistakes he made. He could have opted for an existence filled with misery and crime, but he decided to accept his mistakes and move ahead. He was determined to improve his life and realized that he had to undergo significant changes to achieve the results that he envisioned. His tale tells of forgiveness as well as victory over massive challenges.

The story demonstrates that forgiveness is a decision or process and an approach. It is an internal shift, and it is a personal choice. It takes a lot of hard work, however the mental, physical and psychological benefits from self-forgiveness makes the effort rewarding.

Moving Forward

"Forgive yourself and welcome love back into your life."

-Wayne Dyer

Spiritual teacher and author, Wayne Dyer, gives us an efficient method of thinking in the evening before you go to bed. Instead of using the time to think about the stress from the previous day Dyer suggests to think about what you would like to see within your life. The author says, "...remember you are the final idea that you think about within your head can be stored for at least four hours within the subconscious of your mind. This is four hours of thought programming in just a single minute of reflection prior to entering your subconscious state." If you think about this, it's easy to see the reason why thinking about what you are thinking about before bedtime is crucial.

Small changes like these that can create the most significant change to your daily life. Forgiving yourself is a personal issue, and this guideline outlines a four-week method to guide you towards being capable of forgiving yourself. It's important to recognize that whatever change you decide to undertake must be accompanied for the remainder of your existence. It is a massive transformation in your thinking, but should be mindful to keep up with the latest thoughts and behaviors to ensure that you do be able to avoid old habits. Be sure to stop thinking about them when you realize they could take you in a wrong direction, and remain focused on the present. Being present is the sole power that we possess in any circumstance within our lives.

In her bestselling international publication, You Can Heal Your Life, Louise Hay states: "When we do not move freely right now typically, we're holding onto an earlier time. This could be a feeling of sorrow, regret, grief and fear or guilt or blame, anger even resentment. Sometimes, it's even a desire to take revenge. All of this stems from a state that is unforgiveness or an inability to let go and be present in the current moment. The answer to love is always for healing in any form. The way towards love is forgiveness."

Being able to forgive yourself is such an incredible thing to perform for your mind and body. There are many advantages to forgiveness including:

Being less stressed and/or anxious. The world is filled with an abundance of anxiety and stress. It can also be stressful circumstances. The guilt that comes with guilt may gradually eat away at your body and affect your act. Letting go of the pressure of clinging to events from the past may help ease these issues. When those events are absent, you'll feel more relaxed and worries of the world will not seem as large. When you forgive yourself completely and accept your forgiveness, you're looking forward to enjoying life again. You're feeling renewed and eager to be a part of the joy that is everything. You think you're worthy of another chance to be happy.

Health and cardiovascular health are improved. The heart may take on the burden of a lot as you remember previous injuries. It can lead to issues with your health. Finding peace about your circumstances can improve the overall condition of your heart as well as your overall body. The release of emotional, negative thoughts can strengthen your immune system as well as ease pains and aches as well as give you greater vitality. You'll know whether you've really gone through with it as your body is telling it.

The mental health of people increases.

Forgiving yourself can allow us to be content, rest better and ease us from disorders like post-traumatic stress. The healing of your heart and mind will result from genuine forgiveness. This will give you peace and peace of mind. What person doesn't wish to feel always happy?

It's easier to look at things through a grateful eye. Feeling free from the burden that has been element to your existence for some period of time can bring a surge of joy and enthusiasm that fills you with gratefulness. When you're feeling grateful to the good things that you've got within your life, and decide to look at things with a positive light Many old and worn-out concepts will go away from your life. A motivational speaker Zig Ziglar stated, "Gratitude is the healthiest of human emotions. If you are more grateful for the things you've got and have, the greater chance you'll have more reasons to be grateful for."

Relationships get better.

If you're happy with your self, relationships within your life will benefit. The calm and peace created by forgiveness reduce your stress and make you more productive. So, everyone who is associated with you will be more inclined to cooperate together. A calm and peaceful energy is derived from a peaceful mind. The ability to forgive can help you have peace of mind. It is easier to be a good friend and build lasting relationships.

Spiritual growth improves.

Marcus Aurelius said, "What doesn't transmit light creates its own darkness." It doesn't matter if you're a Christian or not, results of forgiveness could bring about a sense of peace that is awash over you and is a part of your. If you can search within yourself for answers to your difficult issues The result is that you are able to discover the nature of your soul. The true feeling of forgiveness is like a light breeze, tranquil and tranquil, whereas those tumultuous feelings of the issue of unforgiveness are like a burden and are heavy. If you are able to open your mind to the divine power that forgiveness offers, you could discover a side of yourself that you did not know existed.

A few final thought...

What ever you've accomplished, or the time that you've been doing it, you are able to decide to alter your behavior. You can choose whether to endure or not. You can choose to live an existence free from past regret. You have the option of deciding what you do daily basis. You also have the option of choosing to let yourself forgive yourself.

The next method is one that I've never disclosed until recently. It's allowed me to learn to forgive at many times. I would like to aid you in learning to forgive too.

Method: I lie down and take a few deep breaths and allow my body five minutes to process the negative feelings associated with the incident I'm reliving. These emotions include anger, regret or guilt or blame, shame... You know which ones they're. I allow myself the privilege of just five seconds within that negative world or in the world of regret. After those five minutes have passed, I choose to be not living my life that way any longer. I make the choice to forgive. I declare, "I forgive myself for ..." to fill in the empty space. If I'm forgiven by anyone else, I imagine the person I am thinking of and tell them "I forgive you." If I encounter resistance to forgiveness me, I be aware of it and observe the resistance disappear from my mind and body. After that, I feel calm engulfing the situation and then I release and become liberated from the weight which has been weighing me down for the longest time.

It isn't a method suitable for everybody, however when you allow this to work for you, then you'll experience calm. Do we really need to do in this situation? Do we really need to make it that simple? Are we able to let peace? It's impossible to know until you test it.

The world is filled with moments. Certain are great, while others are not so good. But are they? The most important lessons of life are learned through trials and tribulations. One of my close friends once told me "You have to experience what sucks to know what's cool." That is when you choose to label the events that you've had in your life lessons rather than 'failures' they will always be valuable to you. the lessons, and be able to live the life you want to live. In addition, you'll get rid of the past's burdens as well and everyone else who is to you will gain.

Alternative Techniques for Forgiveness and Healing

White Light Meditation

Relax and lie down and without interruptions. Take a moment to close your eyes, and then breathe deeply to relax your mind. Imagine a white, bright illumination in the vicinity in your center. The light can be soothing as well as healing and rejuvenating. As you slowly feel the light start to increase until it encompasses the entirety of your body. Then, you can see it expand beyond the body and create the appearance of a white-colored aura. This light is sure to protect you, bring tranquility in your body as well as uplifting your vibration. Let the light radiate away from your body to the area where you're sitting. The light is cleansing the space around you as it cleanses the body and your soul and even your brain. Feel it healing every organ inside your body. You can feel the increased energy flowing through you that this light exudes across you and around your. Then, you can bring it to you returning to your heart. It fades slowly until it is completely gone However, the energy that emanates from it is still there. Return to your awareness sensations of being awe-inspiring.

Blue and green light meditation

Relieve yourself in a comfortable position, shut your eyes and breathe deeply. Try to relax your body. Think of a stunning glowing green light coming from the area of your solar plexus. It eventually transforms into in a vivid blue after which it alternates between blue and green shades. Imagine these colors filling the body and encompassing every organ, gland and cell. Watch the colors spread into the outside of your body, creating an amazing aura. Green is a color that penetrates the mind to reduce the mood. Blue calms and can help alleviate anxiety. If you are having trouble imagining the hues, imagine the lush green trees and grasses and an uncluttered blue sky or a pool of water. Let yourself soak up the hues to the extent that it makes you feel good. Once you're ready then slowly wrap the light to you then to the region in your solar plexus, until it's gone. Rejoin your consciousness feeling rejuvenated and refreshed.

Deep Breathing Exercise

Relax in a comfortable position or lay down and let your body relax. Inhale deeply through your nose and into your heart. Inhale for 5 seconds and then breathe out through your mouth. Keep your attention on your breathing. If your thoughts wander then gently return it to your breathing. While breathing into your body, picture yourself exhaling white light, bright and pure, unconditional love. Inhale and release all negativity. There may be dark shades appear in your head's eye. Let them go. After ten breaths, allow your breathing to settle and feel peace fill your body. Return to your awareness, feeling revived and refreshed.

Meditation/Visualizations to Remove Negativity

This exercise will help eliminate stored anger as well as anxiety, fear and negative, painful memories.

Relax and unwind. Inhale a few deeply purifying breaths. Relax your eyes, and imagine your image of the grievous moment from the past, as well as the picture that bothers you. Then, imagine a big glass ball and insert this image or event inside the ball. You will be standing in front of the ball of glass. Hold it with your hands and force it to push with enormous force into the ground. You will see it falling into the ground, getting deeper and deeper. Watch as energy cords that connect you to it break and disappear until it is no longer able to hold the power to hold your. After it's gone think of something calming, or happy occurring for your. This could be a hugs from a friend or a smile from someone you love or simply a sense of calm. Relax in the feeling whatever time is needed. After you're finished take a moment to be aware as you feel the warmth within your body.

EFT - Emotional Freedom Technique

The genesis of this practice originated from Chinese practices of acupuncture and Acupressure. While these methods were primarily focussed on the healing of the body from physical problems, a renowned chiropractor under The name of Dr. George Goodheart discovered it may also be beneficial for emotional problems. Dr. Goodheart discovered that tapping specific meridian points could yield positive results.

Over time, different health professionals grew on the research from The late Dr. Goodheart. In the early 1980's, one psychologist, named that of Dr. Roger Callahan discovered that using the technique of meridian tapping when his patient was in the middle of the immediate issue, (such as fear) then the fear would be completely eliminated. Many times, it was permanent. The discovery was made because of a patient that he'd worked with for nearly two years. The patient suffered from an extremely fearful reaction to water, and was unable to shower due to this extreme anxiety. The moment the doctor. Callahan realized this method might help her overcome the fear He thought it was worth the chance. He had her tap specific Meridian points as she talked about the fear she has of water. Then, a remarkable thing took place. She revealed to him that she had no fear! She was skeptical initially, but then she got up and sprinted from the house towards the pool! The pool was a bit too far away and she splashed water onto her face.

Something she'd never had the chance to do prior. Prior to the moment, she'd never ever been allowed to go in the vicinity of a pool. Although it's not as crazy as it could appear, tapping the points of her body during discussions about the issue was able to eliminate her irrational fear. The man who was identified as Gary Craig later developed Dr. Callahan's findings into the Emotional Freedom Technique we know to this day.

EFT can be used for more than just healing anxiety. The numerous benefits that you get through this technique are awe-inspiring. It can help you to be capable of forgiving yourself. If you are struggling with unresolved emotions regarding certain circumstances You might want try giving this method to try. It can help you alleviate or remove old fears, emotions as well as traumas. Although it might seem easy it is actually an effective method to create significant transformations. I frequently use it and find it interesting. It is a fascinating book that discusses the subject, The Tapping Solution by Nick Ortner. It is highly recommended.

Chapter 5: All about Forgiveness

Nearly everyone has experienced the hurt of being injured from a stranger, or those whom he is most concerned about. Unfortunately, the possibility of someone harming you through their words or acts is a matter of unpredictability and unavoidable, since they can happen anytime in the course of one's life. Perhaps your favorite acquaintance decided to not invite you to his party, or your spouse has decided to go out with their group of friends instead of having dinner with you, or your friend stole your idea or perhaps your mother has advised you that you didn't possess the qualities needed to be a decent parent. You may have witnessed someone betraying the trust of you, engaged you in a risky circumstance, or deliberately humiliated you to prove how good they're. Maybe someone has offered you critique that was actually appropriate, but wasn't easy to believe, which is why you disagreed, and then you believed that they had was a thorn in your side. Perhaps someone constantly reminds you of a mistake that you committed, which irritates you.

Whatever motive was of the person who caused you to be offended or hurt the fact is that the act has caused you to feel emotions negatively, which leaves the victim with deep scars and wounds. These injuries are making you experience long-lasting anger, vengeance or even frustration towards the offender.

In the end, you have the option of either you may let anger and resentment to consume you in your life, dictating your feelings and dictate your lifestyle, or you can let yourself learn more about the art of forgiveness, to allow yourself to embrace forgiveness, control your emotions, and get on in your journey.

What exactly is forgiveness?

The majority of people define forgiveness as having the ability to release one's anger, feelings of hatred as well as thoughts of revenge towards those who have done the wrong. A different approach to describe the concept is to recall the incident without feeling feelings of anger, or the urge to take the victim's revenge. The memory is still there, but it isn't a trigger for negative feelings. This means accepting the error as well as the harm that someone else's words, actions or words could have caused.

The majority of psychologists define forgiveness as the conscious and deliberate decision to let go of emotions of anger or resentment towards a person, individual or even someone whom you have hurt, regardless of whether or not they need to be forgiven. This is a choice which you can make to modify how you view your offense (acknowledging the hurt) and an attempt to release all feelings of resentment the hope of gaining an euphoria. The decision to forgive entirely up to you.

What's the definition of forgiveness?

However, the opposite of forgiveness lies the knowledge of what forgiveness actually is. Although forgiveness can heal damaged relationships however, it does not suggest that you are apprehensive about the offense or you'll forget about it entirely. The focus on forgetting an act can lead to denigrating or denying feelings regarding what happened, and this does not mean that you are granting acceptance of forgiveness.

The forgiveness does not excuse the incident and does not suggest that you are willing to suffer the same harm. Giving someone apologies for having caused you harm does not erase any responsibility for the fact that has committed an offense. This does not mean that it is a requirement for you to make a new deal with the person who committed the offense or to release them from any legal responsibility. You can still exercise your legal rights without forgiveness. In the event that justice fails to come through, then you are able to remain in control of whether or not you'd like to be forgiven.

The ability to forgive is still possible without needing to justify any act or statements made. This is simply a means to be a best person. This is the way to getting even the tiniest bit of tranquility that can help to move forward in your daily life.

Do you have a deadline that allows forgiveness?

Giving forgiveness is a difficult task. It can be difficult to comprehend the motives behind why someone committed a wrong. This is particularly in the event that they don't reveal the reasons behind it. Of course, recognizing why these incidents have happened is hard to come by. This requires a lot of contemplating and an extended list of sudden revelations.

The person may need for a long time before the person can declare "I forgive you" or to take it as a fact. A person who has committed mistakes shouldn't count on that the person who made mistakes to forgive the person in an hour or even hours. The process of forgiveness could be long and time can be spent.

What you say or acts that hurt you or make you feel hurt could be viewed in a dark and painful element of your daily life. The negative impact of it could continue in your mind occasionally However, you may slowly lessen the weight of these sad emotions through forgiveness. The act of forgiveness can help you concentrate more on the positive aspects of your life. the one that will lead you to happiness and satisfaction and happiness, which is the only thing that really counts.

Now you know the most fundamentals of forgiveness. But, in order to give forgiveness in the most efficient and full method, you need to understand why it can be beneficial for the health of your body and will help you to have more healthy relationships and leading an enjoyable life. In the end it's a smart choice you have to make if you feel it is the best choice for your needs.

Chapter 6: Why Should You Forgive?

"For if ye forgive men their trespasses, your heavenly Father will also forgive you" Matthew 6:14

It is a sign that someone is a victim of your wrong, and is often accompanied by bitterness and resentments. Forgiveness is often seen as a noble, thoughtful gesture of compassion or a gesture of compassion to someone who caused us to be offended. However, in the end, by allowing forgiveness it is actually beneficial to ourselves. The act of forgiveness can also be crucial in fostering personal growth and can bring amazing positive effects to our overall health and in our social relationships.

Before focusing on the arguments to forgiving, you need to understand the reasons why people have grudges.

What makes holding grudges simple?

If a person you know has caused an act of violence to you, it's normal to hold an anger against the individual. It's quite simple to feel a sense of resentment because in some way, it is an act of vengeance against the individual. The scenario could be replayed through your head and revisit the trauma and suffering that fuels the anger and transforms into exaggerated flames in your head. The resentment you feel is held so that it will keep your anger towards the person who caused an ego that has caused you to offend.

If the people you cherish and respect betray or displease you, it's much easy to harbor an anger as you do not want to be hurt by them. It is expected of them that they will be a loving, caring person for you and prioritize your needs in the same way you would with the people you love. If these expectations aren't fulfilled, and your loved person does exactly the opposite and you feel overwhelmed, depressed and perhaps even disappointed and even betrayed. If one is unhappy and angry, it's normal for them to be unable to stop thinking about the painful events that occurred. The result is feelings of bitterness, anger, and then eventually, the tendency to hold the grievances.

What are the consequences from resenting other people?

I didn't realize the extent to which holding grievances impacted my overall health and interactions with others.

Refusing to accept forgiveness will just cost you more emotionally sense. For those who are not forgiving, they get trapped in bitterness and anger which could negatively impact any future relationships. The people who are unhappy can carry these sentiments of anger and resentment into their the new experiences and relationships which can result in both people ending with a damaged and hurtful relationship prior to being allowed to develop. Someone may feel sad or trapped in the past in which case, they could never fully appreciate the splendor of today. All that can be found in life could seem worthless to an impatient individual.

What are the reasons to learn how to forgive?

Understanding the negative consequences of anger on others could be a source of motivation to you in determining the reasons to forgive. To help you learn more about the reasons why this process ought to be accepted, here are some of the reasons for it:

Inability to forgive can risk your well-being.

If you are encased in the grudge you have, you will tend to remember the event on repeat within your head. In doing this, you be afflicted with negative emotions that are related to the experience. The emotions that are negative that are associated with the incident create anxiety from the memory of the event and can impact the immune system and make your more susceptible to illnesses.

Perhaps you don't realize the moment you are engrossed in the issue, blood pressure and heart rate will increase. The research has managed to establish scientifically the way that it affects our cardiovascular as well as nervous system. It was accomplished by the participants being asked to remember an unpleasant experience, while their blood pressure, heart rates as well as muscle tension were all assessed. In addition, the rates as well as tension and pressure rise, but participants also reported feelings of being less under control (just because they remembered a painful incident that happened during past times). A few people can suffer from a nervous disorder or have episodes of anxiety and/or depression. A few people shed weight or gain it because of the pressure.

However, forgiveness may lower stress levels, which will help you have better immunity. Additionally, forgiveness can reduce blood pressure, and decrease the risk of developing heart attack. The process of forgiveness can help you have lower stress-related health problems.

The reason forgiveness is able to boost your health is due to the fact that after you truly forgive an incident and then you recollect the experience (because forgiveness is possible, but sometimes we don't forget) You no longer suffer from the negative emotions that were associated with the memory. Negative emotions associated with memories can trigger stress, anger, an increase in heart rate in addition to increased blood pressure, and stress that compromise the immunity. When you do accept forgiveness at your own discretion and accept forgiveness, you are free from emotional stress, thus bettering your health, rather than getting out of line to your wellness.

It's just to mention a handful of reasons that a inability to forgive can risk your health. There are many situations which could occur. It is essential to be able to manage yourself to make the safest, most effective and a positive choice on how you can deal with forgiveness.

A lack of forgiveness could prevent people from having fun in their lives.

The thing I discovered about my inability to forgive of forgiveness was that it actually prevented me from having a good time for a long time! This slowed me down from living the life I desired! I was angry with strangers as well as my family and friends who were hurting me. A few people have targeted me for harm but others did not intend to cause harm to me (perhaps I didn't understand). Certain people had shattered my faith, while some had embarrassed me with their criticism of my fears. Certain people have sworn to tell me the truth without a proper manner, and I was not happy with their way of speaking. They squandered my time, and took advantage of my compassion. Others who didn't look after me when they lived were absent from my life to talk about what I was feeling for closure.

The reason for my the lack of forgiveness kept me from having a good time over the years was the fact that I wasn't aware that all I had to do was take the time to understand how to forgive people! If I had spent the time learning the art of forgiveness, I would have not endured so many years filled with anger in my soul. I would have avoided many of the walls that were listening to my grievances, and live an easier life! If I'd taken the time to understand the art of forgiveness and accept their forgiveness, I could have seen that even though I thought I had been wronged by them in one way or another, the grudge that I was holding on to wasn't helping me in any way or aimed at vengeance against the offender (what I believed was the case at the time helped me feel better). Actually keeping grudges actually was keeping me from progress!

My health was being impacted by grudges! My physical health was affected due to the anger I carried around and the relationships I had with my friends were in a state of stress. If I had took the time to study how to forgive people I would have realized that I don't have to allow someone else's behavior however naive, determine my lifestyle! I would've realized that I had to not blame others for my lack of happiness (despite their hurtful actions to me) and be able to take responsibility to my own satisfaction. I would have discovered that there's more to it than my frustration over the incident and I'd have realized that a personal growth plan should be in place, one that includes self-care.

The way I see it now is that the injustice caused to me was in the past. I just needed to let go of living in the past! This doesn't mean I was a fan of what was done to me. This doesn't mean I should be with my perpetrators. Giving them forgiveness didn't mean I would never wounded again. It just signified that I was get rid of the judgement I had against them as a result of their conduct (whether they did me harm intentionally or it wasn't). I wished to be free from the ache I experienced every time I remembered the event. This meant I'd acquired enough forgiveness knowledge to realize that I don't want to carry the bitterness that was residing in my soul that kept my enjoyment of life! This meant that should I want to be able to go on with my life, it was time to understand how to get rid of the unneeded mental burden I carried around.

When I began to discover that I'd in fact been carrying blocks of bitterness around my shoulders (which I was not actively utilizing) I put them down with relief and started to create my own foundations that was based on forgiveness, kindness and the love of God. I was no longer required to dwell on the old past! In my Christian faith it was not my responsibility to punish my wrongdoers. My responsibility lay at the mercy of Jesus Christ to address on my behalf. My obligation was to) learn the lesson of the wrongs I committed by continuing to be a strong advocate for myself through the processes of forgiveness, and 2.) be the person that he had planned for me, by acting as an example for his desires in this day and time.

We'll take a short detour from the reason why it is important to learn how to forgive. Here are a few lessons I've learned from getting hurt by people around me:

Do not allow others to influence your feelings (whether they are trying to harm you intentionally or otherwise). Some people do not intend to hurt your feelings, however some aren't concerned about how you feel. It was my experience that taught me to ask for prayers for people that don't seem to have any issues in hurting my feelings. I'm okay with sending their blessings.

Furthermore I'm not going to be able to let someone else's actions determine my mood. When I was a child, I realized that if a person can cause me to be upset this indicates of something I have to address. So, don't be a victim to others who will stifle your light by causing you to feel dark. What do you know about yourself by watching someone else is causing you trouble?

If I do not understand how to be a good friend and respect me and treat me with respect, there's no reason to stay with this person. So why should I allow anyone an chance to harm me?

There's nothing to cause me to be insecure which anyone can attack since I'm special. I'm unique, and I are perfect even with my shortcomings. Self-healing is a key aspect. There's absolutely no reason to be a victim of doubts or fears. If you can empower yourself and realize what your fears are and how to overcome them, you will recognize how unique, beautiful and exceptional you truly are.

* If a person doesn't have the ability to effectively express their emotions to me, that's fine. I'm not about be bending off my feet. It could be that they're in need of working in their communications abilities. The only thing I can do is concentrate on developing my communication abilities, my ability to comprehend and personal growth so that I lead a happy life and can set an inspiring example.

In the event that anyone is uncaring and/or rude with their interactions with me, I'll be referring to the lesson 2 above. There is no reason to remain with them, or for them to remain with me. It is my responsibility to treat others with respect just the way I treat my fellow humans.

* The only one who allows others to spend my time and profit from my

compassionate character is myself. Thus, since I realize the importance of my own self as a person I am able to love myself as I ought to. I am confident that I won't get angry at people who have abused me previously. In the present, I'm confident I'll never allow anyone else wasted time. Smile.

*I realize that those deceased individuals who have been a part of my life and who didn't properly take care of me during my past years, most likely lived a difficult life for themselves. I am sorry for the lack of care they showed for me may have led to my insecurities (such being unable to love me and other fears) but I do not want to be a victim of the past! They aren't even living! If I do not forgive them, I will not be able to continue living my life. Now I realize the value of what they have done to me. It is evident that I'm a more mature individual because of their actions and I've decided to change my perspective on the world, and not remain a slave to the previous experiences. It is a blessing that I've gained an opportunity to be able to write about and share with other people in the present! Through this experience, I learned that if I could forgiving someone that I am unable to even speak to (who might have committed one of one of the most egregious offenses against me of all) and I am able to accept forgiveness from someone else who is living.

Then, let's look back to other motives to learn to accept forgiveness.

It is important to learn how to forgive, because the strength of forgiveness is in forgiveness.

To forgive implies that you have the courage to let yourself understand the reason for bad events, and also to acknowledge that the past will never ever be altered. When you are strong, it is also brave and forgiving means you have the courage to offer the relationship a new opportunity or maybe you're courageous enough to allow yourself the possibility of enjoying the rest of your life (without any other person being living in the way). You're brave enough to allow the other person the chance to grow into a more successful and more responsible within your own life, or maybe you're brave enough to accept their forgiveness and let them lead with peace of mind and free from any harm that they have caused to you.

A few people are not happy with forgiveness due to the fact that they believe it gives the perpetrator the opportunity to have an "easy way out" while those who have been hurt suffer with the painful memory of the incident. Some believe that forgiveness demands that you forget everything that occurred. However, this isn't the case Most experts in forgiveness realize that it requires a lot of courage and patience to heal to overcome the anger and bitterness. The act of forgiveness is not a way to erase memories. It is a decision made with complete confidence to release the burden of painful memories to allow you to go on to enjoy the happiness of a wonderful and fulfilled life. Keep in mind that you are the one who must live with the choice to forgive, this is a decision you take.

It is important to learn how to forgive since you are given the ability to forgive.

The majority of the time, the decision to refuse to let go of anger is that he or isn't ready to or is not capable of doing so simply because they are unable to. Each human being is endowed with the ability to forgive people who did his or her wrong. However, it could take some patience, strength and courage for one to do this. Unforgiveness puts the potential you've been blessed with into a squandering state and takes away the ability to live life through resentment.

It is important to learn how to forgive, as forgiveness is an act of kindness can be given to yourself.

The process of accepting forgiveness and embracing forgiveness not just helps the person whom you've forgiving, but also you. It is actually yourself and your needs which will reap the greatest benefits through this process. The ability to forgive frees from all the tension that you experience.

It lets you regain your peace of mind that you experienced before another individual did something to caused you pain. Accepting forgiveness allows you to enter in new friendships without having to carry through all the negative things that have happened through the years.

Learn to forgive, as it gives the peace of your mind.

If you are able to release all anger you feel towards individuals who did the wrong thing, you'll get back your calmness that you used to have. To forgive yourself, you are free of those grudges or guilt you have and cause your frustrations and confusion that you experience in your daily life.

Giving someone else the benefit of the doubt for a mistakes that he/she did in a way allows you to let everything go which allows you to concentrate on what is important rather than the things that matter. This also helps you feel more satisfied and allows you to be able to feel calm, understanding optimism, and the ability to be more likable to others.

Learn to forgive because when you can forgive yourself, you're granting yourself the right to live life to the maximum.

Being able to live life to the fullest means happiness and fulfillment. To attain this goal, you need get rid of any negative feeling you may have Examples of this include the bitterness of anger as well as bitterness.

Each person is given a decision. You can decide either to be satisfied and content, or keep regrets and grudges. In the absence of letting the things that make you be angry and sad and unhappy, it's impossible to become completely content and serene. It is impossible to live your life in the that you wish to because the negative feelings keep taking you away.

If you want to live a more fulfilling existence, allow yourself to understand how to be kind to others, and implement the lessons learned to your life, as well as the relationships you have with your friends.

When we are hurt by someone else and we have an animosity towards those who have hurt us, we assist in being a bit uncooperative or with people we later come across in our lives that are not like the individuals who have caused us pain, thereby affecting our relationships with other people and capability to live life fully. The ability to let loose the weights which weigh you down could help you to live a more fulfilling life. It can help you get away without the resentments brought on from the loss. In the absence of these negative emotions and resentments, you will be more content as well as more tranquil and more satisfied.

The concept of forgiveness is worth using in every aspect of our lives. That includes relationships with families and in marriage, as well as with coworkers, friends as well as with strangers. It improves our connections and acts as a source of kindness. If you've developed better social relationships with people around you and are more likely to live life in the best way possible. It is only through forgiveness that you are able to rid yourself of these issues and this is achieved through learning to let go of the past.

It is important to learn to forgive, as it will allow you to view every individual you meet as an educator.

You may not wish to look at the situation this way, as being grieving and experiencing sadness and frustrations doesn't seem to be a good time to learn something from the offender. However, through these circumstances (which that you never asked to experience) you can learn a few aspects, such as the right way to respond or how to respond when the scenario arises in the future. You did not wish for this situation to arise, however, in the real world, it's important to look at the lessons you can take from such unfortunate events.

When I was a teenager I've been upset with certain people that were supposed to offer me an ordinary childhood. In particular, there were certain individuals who have passed away. Before I was taught how to forgive, I didn't realized how much they had actually taught me through the midst of those unhappiness situations. We can say I'm describing my process of healing and releasing myself from one of the things which held me back many years, and that was my frustration. I'm not responsible any longer. I am determined to make a change and stop living in the past. I'm completely content with the way I am. I am free.

Being able to accept forgiveness can allow you to look at all the bad experiences as lessons consider other people as educators - those that have the potential of instructing you about your life. Through understanding and accepting the wrongs done by another person to you, and finally allowing them to be forgiven and moving through your day. Should such incidents occur again at some point in the near future you'll already have the necessary knowledge to manage the situation correctly, thanks to the blessings given those who forgive you through the ability of forgiveness.

Learn to forgive since it's this, you will get rid of the hold of anger.

In forgiveness, you are freed, more especially your emotions, of someone else who is controlling you. What I mean is that the anger you experience as a result of the actions of someone else effectively controls your. This anger prevents you from living a happy life since when you think about how it happened, you're likely to replay the anger that is attached to the incident. When you accept forgiveness and release anger, it allows you the chance to enjoy your life as you would like to. You are no longer an unending victim of anger.

It is important to learn how to forgive since everyone makes errors.

Sometime in the course of your existence, you may had the chance to harm people you love too. The reason for this is in the famous phrase "What goes around comes around".

While I'm not suggesting that if your actions have caused harm to anyone that you should be hurt again, but I'm saying that when you've injured someone (and there is a good chance that you've committed this once or twice throughout your life) I'm certain you'd like to be pardoned.

Humans are all prone to doing things that no other human can do unimaginable and unimaginable things.

due to this, each human being is begging to receive the same level of forgiveness. Giving others forgiveness for the things they've done to them takes away the guilt as well as the consequences that come with such words and acts. When you forgive others it also helps make a space in your brain that allows you to accept the consequences of your unthinking acts towards other people as well. As you'd like to have forgiveness, you should also the people around you.

Learn to forgive, as it opens the door to an entirely different kind of affection.

It lets you forget about the past and take a step forward for the best future. While letting go of the past doesn't automatically suggest that you must give up the relation too.

The decision to forgive your beloved one can be a sign that you're ready to give them an opportunity to try again. This could mean that, this time, you're prepared to make a risk as well as reclaim the faith you felt for your partner. This allows you to go on into the next chapter in your life together.

An incident like this could enhance the bond you are in. Stronger relationships will permit the person to pour more affection in it. And with the new amount of love put into it, you can feel certain that your beloved one will be more cautious in their conduct or actions. It is only you who will feel the warmth of your heart that this is possible.

Chapter 7: How to Forgive

"To forgive is to set a prisoner free and discover that the prisoner was you." - Lewis B. Smedes

Giving forgiveness to others is difficult and demanding. Some might seem difficult, or even absurd. If you are empowered and have determination, as well as accepting and understanding, forgiveness for an individual could be straightforward enough.

As we grow in this part in our life, we start to observe a shift in our thought process. As we grow, we develop as more compassionate human beings. The result is more respect. Our self-esteem improves and learn the ways to recognize situations that might be harmful to us, before they occur. Our lives can be enriched by happier situations. It is possible to surround ourselves with loving people but it takes patience. Here are some crucial steps to guide you along the way to experience the true healing power of forgiveness

Let yourself be empowered to accept forgiveness.

The ability to forgive others is an ongoing learning process. This is for you to read this text now. You want to know the best way to be able to forgive someone else.

In the beginning of my quest towards learning how to forgive other people I read up on a ton of books on the subject. However, it wasn't until I experienced my realization that I knew why it was crucial that I accept forgiveness from others. The reason for my epiphany was that I continued to empower myself on this subject. Within my religion, I was struggling with forgiveness. For me personally, if I'd been more focused on my Bible when I was struggling I might have received all the answers I sought, but what I'm trying to get across is that the journey you are on isn't over. Continue to be studying and learning about the method. Once you're ready accept forgiveness, you'll know that.

Let go when you're at your best.

The process of forgiveness for someone else is not to be taken lightly. It's fine if it can take a long time before you're prepared to forgive the other person. Let them go when you're prepared because it's important your chance to be happier.

In the past, forgiving isn't a sign that you agree with any wrongdoing. Nor is it a guarantee that you'll forget about it completely. It is not a way to excuse the crime, or mean you accept that you will be hurt in the future. Also, it does not obligate you to reconcile with the perpetrator/s. The decision that you take to recognize the pain you feel and to make it is a conscious effort to shed all feelings of anger within your soul in order to achieve calm mind. The decision to forgive entirely up to you

Take a moment to learn from the stories of forgiveness from other people.

Take a look around and find individuals who've been in the exact same situation as you currently. Consider the things they had to do when in your position - what they did to be able to forgive the mistakes made to them and the ways they dealt with their anger.

Every person's experience is unique. Certain people may attend counseling sessions to connect with those who shared the same experiences. Many people prefer doing research on the internet to find others who have dealt through a certain issue. Watching others release of their resentment is a good method to see how they have managed to conquer their issues. The joy they feel when they are free of their burdens could prove an inspiration to you.

I was recently watching the film that was based on an actual account that delivered a profound message for me. A child was entrapped by a terrorist group that required him to murder his mother right in a matter of minutes or else the mother of his younger brother were shot right in front of the group. The child was saved from the terrorist organization and was placed in a refugee place with kids who were saved from similar circumstances. The rescuer tried repeatedly to speak with him and get in touch with his son, but the boy could not even talk to him. His rescuer was dealing with serious concerns and was in a state of stress. He could see that the rescuer was unprepared due to the pressure. He decided to speak with his rescuer and share his experience for the first time. A powerful message was delivered as the boy concluded his account by saying that regardless of what happened to him after being taken away, he realized that he was not going to allow "them" (the terrorists) to take away his heart. The boy had learnt to forgive, and took away his heart from the hurt that came as consequence of the horrific incident that occurred to him!

Perhaps the pain that someone else may cause you is a sensitive issue to the way you feel. You might feel like nobody will be able to understand. If other people can help you to find a way to conquer your fears accept their stories. Engage in any positive behavior you feel comfortable doing so that you can be motivated to let go.

Take the time to look at the entire narrative, as well as to consider all sides of the story.

In the event that it's not an easy to determine the facts Try to consider all sides. Each story is a tale with two sides: yours as well as the perspective of another person (and in certain cases, there may be three sides, you, them and the truth). Find out what caused the person to have made the mistake. Take into consideration every aspect which could lead to what you have done. If you can see things that the other person is looking at and you can be more accepting. Particularly if you realize that the person who hurt you was not attempting to harm you, and the accident was completely accidental.

That's where communication is crucial. There are times when we might be hurt by a ineffective communication. It is a great relief when we are capable of identifying the issue and rectify the issue.

Try to consider every element of the incident - like the way you've responded to it, and the words you were able to say as a result. Then, consider how these events have had the potential to influence your life after.

By doing both, it will enable you to learn the lessons you ought to have absorbed from the incident. After you've been in a position to take these lessons into consideration lessons, you will be able to manage situations better in the event that it occurs again. What do you think about the incident and how did it happen that you were offended by? Perhaps you'd want to speak with anyone you trust about the incident?

Then you should be able to go on.

If you decide to accept or reject forgiveness but one thing is that is for sure: you need to be able to continue and live your life (you must not keep a tin of the anger). It is not advisable to dwell on your past. Additionally, your past is not a reason for your self-destruct at the moment. Concentrate on the present as well as the factors you value and focus on your ideal lifestyle that includes letting go of negativity from your past.

Try to put your focus to find a new option to achieve your objectives than by focusing on the incident that hurt you. Do your best to assist yourself in the process of getting rid of the past, make sure it doesn't come back to repeat itself and work at your ritm.

Don't expect too much from people around you as they might not provide you with what you want (perhaps assistance, compassion or perhaps the opportunity to apologize). Make sure you are seeking love, wellbeing good relationships and prosperity in the wake of your experiences. Concentrate on understanding the procedure and knowing the speed you need to go to heal properly. At some point, you'll be able to change how you look at your life's events so that you are able to remember and be inspired by the courage you took to make a change and forget what happened.

Remind yourself that forgiveness doesn't suggest that you have accepted the wrong conduct, nor does it mean that need to engage with someone who purposely injured your feelings. If someone has not given a sincere apology, or has provided you with an unworthy apology, there's nothing to force you to view the person as trustworthy. Nor is it necessary to become the victim to further negative treatment. Move to the next step.

Chapter 8: Consider Whether Your Resentment Is Justified or Not

In the first place, your process of getting rid of anger out of your relationship demands reflection. Before taking steps towards making an effort to forgive your partner for any shortcomings that you consider within them, it's important to look at the way you feel about yourself and how you feel. Determine reasons you're feeling angry towards your companion. Does your anger stem from some of the actions they took by them? Are they based on an event they did or didn't perform, or on a statement they've said or did, or based on what you believe they committed?

The first inquiry you should ask yourself is "Is my resentment justified?" A truthful answer to this question can give you a good understanding of whether the root cause is in your relationship partner, or manner in which you both developed your relationships.

If not then think about why your feel this way, and the reason you're blaming your spouse. It could be that you are feeling unworthy and directing your anger on your partner instead of trying on resolving your issues. Maybe there's another issue that is affecting your life that you're all-but-involved in channeling your frustration towards your partner, instead of someone who truly is the one who deserves the blame. You might also find yourself in a difficult circumstance in your life something you're unable to solve as you don't have anyone accountable, you place your anger on your partner.

If you can honestly say yes, then your resentment can be justified. It is crucial to know the areas in which your spouse has failed or isn't meeting your expectations. The reasons for their failures could range from attention-deficit or disrespect to worrying things like having a relationship that is not dependable. If they're in the worst-case scenario the person is physically or verbally inflicting harm. Although cheating might or might not constitute a major issue, abusive behavior shouldn't be allowed to continue. If you witness violence or abuse of any kind and you are unable to leave the danger zone and end any contact with your spouse.

When it comes to deal breakers it is also important decide if what frustrates you with your spouse or their conduct is unacceptable to you. It is up to you to determine whether or not it's possible to maintain a positive relationship based on these conditions.

The most heated issues when it comes to breaking up relationships is cheating. Cheating is among the most common causes of anger among partners, and also one of the most risky issues if left unaddressed. The inability to discuss it, and then coming to an agreement on the issue with each other, whether that's keeping the relationship or ending it and causing resentment, is a sure way to create. This could lead to discontent as well as a more unpleasant ending over the long run.

If it's something you do not want to be associated with take the time to be truthful and acknowledge that your relationship is on a course. There's no need to cause damage to your loved one in trying to keep a relationship in existence. If you're unable to accept their apology and are not able to envision an opportunity to be together in the near future It's the right time to stop the relationship. Perhaps, you're more patient and are willful to forgive or consider that the motives of your partner to betray you were legitimate. Maybe, you think that this was an isolated incident and it wasn't an issue that was serious. Whatever the reason discuss the issue openly transpired and find out your partner's motives and opinions about the incident. It is possible to come to an agreement by establishing a healthy relationship. Though self-analysis and reflection is useful, taking your feelings downwards isn't. Only when you are able to communicate openly from both sides can really achieve a constructive resolution to a conflict between two people and find the real'resentment remedy'.

Chapter 9: Talk to your partner about your resentment

Much like most other things the issue is addressed most effectively by having transparent, open communicating. Many times the person you are talking to may not know they're making a mistake or their behavior or attitude is an area of frustration and discontent for the two of you. It's essential that you're transparent about your feelings about what's bothering you, and stay open to dialogue.

Make sure to not appear excessively negative - this can only lead your spouse to get defensive, and it will be difficult to express your feelings effectively. that is bothering you. Expressing your emotions and listening to your companion in the same way are equally essential in bringing about an effective resolution to your dispute. Communication is a two-way street and recollecting this will spare the two of you heartache and anger.

If you can explain how you feel as well as the ways your partner can contribute to it will aid them in understanding the way you feel. Your partner will have the chance to place themselves within your position. They will be compelled to modify their behavior in line with your expectations. They can also be able to explain why they behaved the way they did and how they did not know the way you feel regarding the incident. In the past, careful monitoring both parties is crucial. Negative attitude or failing to consider the situation seriously can lead to more unhappy feelings and unresolved emotions that can lead to anger.

Also, you must convey your feelings in a non-demeaning manner you can.

However, at also, do not hesitate to speak up that they're making you or caused you to feel uncomfortable or insecure and the way that it has led to the bitterness you feel. The act of gloating over your emotional issues or hurt feelings won't help you resolve this issue or in any way. In addition, it's unfair for both you and your spouse, as they will not be able to alter their mindset or alter situations if they do not be aware of the severity of the problem.

Begin the discussion in a period when you're both calm and are not feeling stressed or other pressure from outside. Engaging in a discussion like this late after dark or when both either exhausted or stressed out from work likely to not lead to an effective discussion or bring satisfactory result. You should instead approach your partner early in the morning or during the weekend in an environment where both of you are comfortable. You should ensure that there is plenty of time to chat as what you don't want is to start an argument prior to going to work, only to return to home more bitter and angry with one another. Allow yourself time to discuss your feelings, talk to one another and figure issues out.

Take it on with a clear mind and be confident that your spouse will be willing to compromise or acknowledge their error and apologize. Becoming aware of their concerns will result in better outcomes instead of ignoring it. The elimination of any disagreements which may have occurred between both of you is the first stage towards forgiveness and making the mistake of not remembering that it was ever a reality. Honest communication is the most effective solution for any problem that arises between two people, particularly in the context of a relationship. It is impossible to forgive without honesty and the desire to grant the forgiveness.

Chapter 10: Expression Instead of Suppression

The chapter could be titled "Get Angry", because it's what I'm trying to promote. It's not a good idea to always be angry or at random times however, if you feel unhappiness or frustration are justified be sure to communicate these feelings to your spouse immediately and without hesitation. Explain in detail the reason you are feeling this way. This is in line with the previous section on communications, however this is much more focused on communicating on instantaneously, when the topic is important, and not the future.

The ability to express your feelings about negative things is good for you and improves your relationship. Being afraid to look negative can cause you to suppress the emotions. In turn, repressing emotion can lead to resentment. On the other hand, the act of expressing them provides you with an opportunity to resolve your issue in the way it unfolds. If you are able to express your feelings in a clear and honest manner, it does not allow for hidden emotions of anger which can be a source of stress and damage to you as well as your relationship.

It's a good idea to think about this - venting your frustration is liberating, and emotions that are negative are as important as those that are positive. It is not acceptable to feel embarrassed for being angry, sad or frustrated in any manner of feeling; they are designed to be expressed, not stored away in. The act of letting negative emotions accumulate in your mind means that you'll examine them and spend a lot of time dissecting them. The result is that you'll be angry for a longer period of time than is necessary. The act of avoiding anger creates frustration. It also can cause you to view things in a defiant manner. It's not good for any person - certainly not yourself and certainly not your spouse. These bad feelings can turn into, guess what? the term, long-term anger.

Additionally the fact that you aren't telling your partner what you think could seem unfair which, in turn, could create the impression that they've been misled. Resentment that is held for an extended period of time only to speak it out later could cause your spouse to be overwhelmed, confused and even defensive. Then they're confronted with an array of allegations as well as hidden emotions that were not aware of prior to - difficult to manage. It's actually very difficult for even those who are the most well-adjusted that is why it can trigger people to take retaliation. The result is sure to escalate the tension and cause more problems than they are already.

Women in particular are guilty of hiding their feelings particularly anger. It is due to the fact that within many different cultures, women are taught to accept and be tolerant to their peers and place them and their opinions first. In conjunction with the illogical notion that anger isn't "lady-like", repression does much harm but does nothing positive. Males, on their own are usually allowed and encouraged to show an anger since it's perceived as a characteristic of masculinity. However, many societies ridicule men for showing sadness or being emotionally 'humble'. They hide these emotions because they fear appearing as weak or lacking in masculinity that doesn't serve them much good especially in relationships.

Therefore, even though repression can be not gender-specific, it is a common practice by both genders because of different reasons. Also, it is harmful for everyone whatever gender. In addition, the practice of repressing emotion is not a good strategy for dealing with relationships between people. It's a great source of anger toward each other.

The process of forgiveness is much easier and gained by venting your emotions and resolving your situation immediately. Speaking openly and honestly about the emotions you are feeling isn't negative, it's actually useful in dispersing negative scenario. When you allow negative thoughts to sit for a long duration the thoughts can alter your perspective of events and can trigger emotions that get blown over the top.

Chapter 11: Let It Go and Move On

When you've sorted things out with your partner and taken the first step towards a solution to your problems, there's an absolute requirement you have to accomplish - release it. That is, when the issues are resolved you must stop focusing on your past, and continue in your daily life and relationship.

For true forgiveness, it's impossible without forgetting, and it depends upon not dwelling on the previous events. If you've chosen to forgive and forget, and have communicated it to your spouse not to dwell on the past negativity isn't fair. It's unjust to you and your partner. This is not only negative to your personal well-being as well, it will affect your whole relationship. If you continue to think about the many reasons why you dislike your partner even when you've discussed and concluded the issue, results in unnecessary hurt. The only thing it does is trigger your emotions of anger repeatedly over and over that is not good for you or your partner. This anger can eventually transform into resentment, and could end your relationship.

The choice to forget and forgive signals an adult, well-balanced person. As a sign of stability and maturity You must realize that you'll never be able to erase your anger without removing the source. If you've made it to this point this means that you've found the root of your resentment and responded in the right way by speaking to your spouse about the issue. After you've gotten to the source of the problem and resolved the conflict and gotten the conflict removed. In this moment, the most challenging steps have been accomplished.

But, that doesn't suggest that the present process of forgiveness and forget isn't simple or less significant over the other steps. Each step will help you achieve the goal of getting rid from resentments and feelings and anger. None of them can be ignored.

Everyone knows that getting over it is more easily thought of than actually doing. We know that emotions occur on their own and are not always in control, you can influence your reaction to thoughts or issues that cause them.

This may seem as if it's a complicated and difficult method, but it's really not difficult. It's just a matter of making an effort to not be thinking about the triggers that brought on those negative emotions. Don't let them upset you. As with everything that are difficult in the beginning, but it gets quicker with experience and repetition. As you progress, you'll become familiar with responding to certain situations differently that you did in the past. When you can rationally realize that you've resolved the issue with your spouse and gotten over your anger and emotions, it becomes much easier to manage the emotional reaction.

Willpower is the main force here, along with the desire to build your relationship, and to truly forgive your spouse. The release of previous anger will be a relief for you, an individual. It will make a huge difference to your relationship. A positive outlook and ability to compromise can bring about a brighter outlook of your partnership. The ability to compromise is vital for the health of your relationship. Being in control of your emotions will be one of the most beneficial actions you've made for your self. You'll never become a slave to your emotions, no matter how you feel they're unjustified or unreasonable.

Chapter 12: Focusing On the Positive

The last part of your path to forgiveness is not to focus on the past, but instead looks forward to the future, which is a more positive and more enjoyable one. This is a way to help those who have accepted forgiveness and healed their wounds. The ones who have decided to let go of their memories and negative emotions so that they can focus upon the good.

A positive outlook is the most common advice which is often neglected. But it's an vital part of recovery process. This doesn't mean that you need to change your appearance and turn into optimistic, even if it's your personality or who you wish to become, but I'm talking about looking at things that are positive about your relationship.

The feelings that you've failed to get rid of need to be replaced by more positive emotions. I suggest you try to find and pinpoint your top qualities concerning your spouse and the relationship you have with them. Recall the beginning: which aspect of your partner enticed you to begin with and how have been a beneficial influence in your daily life? Take a look at the smallest aspects that helped you feel awestruck by your partner and which help keep the relationship alive. The old saying "In with the good and out with the bad" isn't a lie and can be of huge help to you in your recovery process.

After spending a specific length of time with a person, we can begin to see them as being as a given. We don't appreciate them as much as that we did before or perhaps we do not show that appreciation. It becomes apparent that your spouse recognizes your appreciation without having to express that. It is an easy method of generating resentment since people are emotional creatures that require to be valued and loved - constant evidence in the form of words and actions will always be appreciated. An inability to consistently express love and appreciation, or experiencing a time filled with resentment can create a difficult time remembering the things that made your relationship satisfying initially. It is therefore crucial to put in the effort not to just forgive and forget about your loved ones however, you should always communicate to them your appreciation to your partner. This can lead to strengthening the relationship between you.

In reality, everyone needs reassurance in every aspect of our lives, especially when it comes to a relationship. The relationship must be maintained equal by all the those involved, and reassurance is an important role in this. It demonstrates trust, respect and respect for the relationship, and shows that you've really overcome your disagreements to a more positive future for your spouse.

Chapter 13: The Offender Does Not Acknowledge Your Hurt

There are many possible reasons for why you might be not willing or able to let go of someone who has hurt you in the worst way. Once you know the reason of this resistance, it is easier to come up with an answer. Another reason could be that diagnosing causes an answer.

Apologizing and forgiving

If you are offended by someone You expect them to not just to admit the fact that they hurt you but also demonstrate that they are sincere in their apology. It is your belief that you are worthy of this and more given the terrible repercussions are awaiting you. It is not difficult to see that there can be valid reasons for the reluctance of you to be forgiven. It is then a question of does my forgiveness have to be based on an apology as well as my belief that they truly regret their actions? The Bible is not one of these as a prerequisite to forgive an offender.

It is your duty to be able to forgive them regardless of whether they have apologized or otherwise. It's appropriate and biblical to tell them the extent to which they hurt you. There are some who will apologize but others may not.

People will never apologize for their mistakes.

They might not be apologizing due to the fear that they could use the apology against them.

There are those who have experienced bad experiences at some point in their lives, when those who apologized to them was a source of embarrassment in some manner.

Many people aren't sure what to say about their regret and are not accustomed to do so.

Certain people will be apologetic through the actions they took, perhaps give you a gift or use other methods to show their regret and apologize. Get down to their level. Accept the situation. But if they will refuse, or if all sources are exhausted, then you must obey God and to be forgiven.

There are many reasons some people aren't inclined to be sorry, but do not let these deter the possibility of being open to forgiveness. Your emotions as well as your needs aside so that you can obey the rules of your superior. Jesus Christ, your Primary model, never expected to see the Pharisees to kneel before Him and begging for forgiveness for their transgressions. When He was crucified,

He was being slammed by His adversaries, and as they were deciding over who should inherit his clothing, He asked for forgiveness from them.

And he said to Jesus"Father, let them go; they do not know the things they are doing. Then they separated his raiment and threw many lots (Luke 23:34).

Be aware that forgiveness isn't just for the offender but is for you since you desire to be pleasing to God and you desire to benefit from forgiveness. For a reminder, when giving up others in the name of the believer, it secures the forgiveness of your own, and lets you be free of emotional turmoil including anger, hurt feelings, bitterness and the like. The positive aspect is that you can feel the relief which forgiveness can bring. Keep in mind that forgiveness is solely with you as well as God. The offender doesn't have to participate with this only to relieve them of their suffering and ensure them that they have been forgiven. There are some who don't care whether you accept their forgiveness or you don't. However, you must be concerned that you don't forfeit the benefits of forgiveness as a result the other person's "I don't care" attitude. You are to follow the Lord.

The mystery of the LORD (is) with the people who trust in him. He will reveal to his covenant to them (Psalms 25:14).

Recognizing and reconciling

One reason you might not wish to be forgiven is because it is possible to mistake forgiveness for reconciliation. Although God's forgiveness can lead to the automatic reconciliation of people, our forgiveness may not always bring about reconciliation. There is no obligation to reconcile with your adversary if their relationship is a toxic one and volatile, or when they refuse to make changes in their behaviour. What we must do is to accept their forgiveness, in order to stop holding the anger, hatred or bitterness towards them. The difference is.

The principle of forgiveness is unidirectional. The obligation is to forgive regardless of another person's actions. However, reconciliation operates according to a different tenet.

Do two persons walk with each other with the exception of a mutual agreement? (Amos 3:3)

To allow reconciliation for reconciliation to take place, both of you have to agree on a set of terms regarding how you can avoid repeating an offense later on. If, for instance, someone you know always makes you look embarrassed when you are out in public due to his rough manner of conduct or his acquaintance with you, then you should never take him out any further unless you promise him that he won't cause you to embarrassment in the future. If he does not make that promise and offers the excuse that he wishes to be able to behave however he wants or claims that you're too sensitive, then you can take precautions by avoiding having a night out with them, but this does not necessarily mean you ending of your relationship. If you go out this, it could represent a show of ill-will as well as a retaliation. It is possible to continue the friendship you have with us without putting ourselves at risk.

For a summary to sum up, your forgiveness should not be dependent on the apology offered by your perpetrator. You accept their forgiveness regardless of the response. By letting them go you're the one to benefit from the experience. Do not wish for the blessings you receive to go unnoticed as you wait for an apology which may not ever come. Follow following the example of Jesus Christ, who forgiven His sinners and did not wait for an apology. You are forgiven because much depends upon it.

If you are praying to God, be forgiven if you need to be against anyone, That your Father who is in heaven will accept your forgiveness for sins (Mark 11:25).

Forgiveness Prayer

Lord, please help me be patient even when my offender don't admit to their sins. Keep my eyes on You as the one I must obey. I pray that my fear of you overpower their lack of remorse or apology. If my resolve is weak I will be able to forgive them for their sins, no matter how hard it might be and in Jesus in Jesus' name.

We Live With the Consequences

One of the most important reason we don't want to be forgiven is that we are forced to deal in the aftermath of the incident. These consequences can take many types, yet each day, we're faced in pain. It is a painful experience that we have to bear all the time.

The consequences of suffering

The suffering and pain that comes due to the actions of our perpetrator is twice as difficult to accept their forgiveness. It's hard to accept the responsibility of the individual who was the person we gave authority to manage the finances of our household. The person, with our ignorance and our consent, manipulated our money and evaded the remainder. The damage is irreparable.

The consequences of a crime do not always come as physical discomfort or limitations Some come in as emotional pain which we could face each day. How can I accept James the person who murdered all my children while drunk? The passage of time cannot restore my husband, two sons, and my sole daughter. The excitement of watching the couple marry and become an aunt is over. It was supposed that they would have laid me to rest, however it's the reverse situation. They had to be buried.. How can I let him know that I am guilty of depriving myself of my husband, when I'm just 32? What can I do to forgive the person who caused many hurts in my life?

Social Consequences

Sometimes it is the case that the crime can lead to social repercussions. Certain people's actions can put us in a situation. The name of our company is gone, the reputation of our company is damaged. Somebody lied about us, and that lingered on the minds of many for a number of years. Someone shared confidential data about us, which caused us irreparable harm. What could Joseph accept his brothers' guilt who sold him to slave markets in which he not only physically assaulted, but was treated no more than other animals? Why would my family and friends be able to leave me, say after everyone been against me?

There are a myriad of consequences of committing an offense. A few of these can be irreparable and we are not as if we can let go. In any way.

God can change the course of events around

The thing that we can count on God with is knowing that God can create some good from every difficult circumstance. God can make it an opportunity to show us how good we are or bring something wonderful from it. When we consider the consequences and think we've lost our way, that may not be so. The consequences can guide us towards understanding our mission in Earth.

Joseph was sold to a slave trader before he was finally able to settle in Egypt. It was possible that he thought the end of his story was near, however, this wasn't the reality. This was the route that led him to be the first President of Egypt.

Later years later, many years later, Lord sent me a message of forgiveness. Drawing inspiration from my own experience of forgiveness I received from the young man who took my family from me I was able to inspire people to forgiving their perpetrators. Many people believe that when I forgive myself to this degree, then they will also be able to forgive perpetrators who did not commit lesser crimes. God has changed my life to the right direction by demonstrating an model of forgiveness to other people. When I read that my story and story have served as a blessing for others that I'm happy and content.

God transformed his story about Joseph around. God changed his story about Job to the upside when he offered Job twice the amount he received previously and blessed him with longevity. Job's story continues to inspire an opportunity to many today.

The LORD changed the fate of Job as he offered prayers for his fellows: additionally, the LORD granted Job double the amount the previous time. Then Job lived Job over a period of one century and forty years and he saw his sons and sons of his even the fourth generation (Job 42:10-16).

He rewrote the tale of David and turned him into the king despite Saul's constant efforts to take him down. If we aren't able to see an immediate turnaround in our circumstance but we are able to still believe in Jesus. You can be forgiven. It is important not to allow the effects we suffer keep us from accepting the forgiveness of our perpetrators.

Don't focus on the negative consequences. Concentrate on the positives and believe in God to turn the situation around. Forgive them and return towards God. Perhaps you are looking at the blessings that been derived from the incident. This could mean that we have a better understanding of how to tackle other significant issues that arise in life. Perhaps God intends to work through our lives in ways that would have never taken place without it occurring to us. Naturally, it's not God who caused us to commit sin and we are aware God is the one who has control.

If we are able to forgive despite the consequences, it is offering God the chance to change the world around for our benefit.

It is also known that everything works to bring good luck to those who are in love with God and to those that are chosen according to his goal (Romans 8:28).

Chapter 14: Forgiveness Prayer

Lord, I believe God is in charge in my daily life. I ask you to help me focus less on the effects of the things that people have done to me. Lord, my focus is focused on You. You are able for this to be a manifestation of the glory of your name.

Being Taken for Granted

Each day we face opportunities to not forgive. Being aware of the motives for us to forgive is helpful as it allows us overcome the obstacles that hinder forgiveness. For instance, we are facing the risk of being viewed as a victim. It's part of our tendency to cheat in order to escape the consequences. Knowing what we're up against and what we can expect, we're better equipped.

Possibility of being taken as granted

One reason that we don't wish to forget is the chance of being assumed to be a given. This isn't just possible and possible. The person who hurt us was at first, but we sincerely apologized to the offender. We let the incident go without regrets. He then rubbed us wrong again and we repaid him. Third time, he committed the same thing, and as with before, we have forgiven the offender. There is the pattern is beginning to emerge.

Certain people will look for opportunities to make money off of our vulnerability. They will begin to think of our blessings as a given. But, the Scriptures that we must forgive seven times seven. Do we allow ourselves to continue to forgive with no fear of the offender having to face penalties and suffering repeatedly or are we exhausted of not letting him go and choose to show him something he'll never forget? It's not the best option. The one thing we should be aware of is the necessity of forgiveness (Ecclesiastes 5:8).

Utilizing wisdom

God does not want us to suffer abuse repeatedly when there is a way to stop the abuse from happening. God is aware of everything and will be there to us. There are actions we need to be taking to prevent the abuse that our perpetrators can inflict on us. Make use of wisdom.

The most important factor; therefore, you should acquire knowledge and the wisdom you gain, develop the ability to comprehend (Proverbs 4:17).

One scenario could be the sharing of our personal prayer requests with our dearest friend. We might have shared the family secrets with her as well as the steps we're taking towards resolving the issue. Then, she opened up about it at a meeting of prayer and revealed a secret that was kept secret. We do talk with her about it. It is likely that she will apologize, however we need to be able to forgive her, even if she doesn't see anything incorrect with the situation. We must, however, take care not to discuss the details of our requests to her again in the near future. The point is that we employ knowledge to prevent use or abuse of our relationship. It also reduces the risk of danger of abuse that we could confront. God is not angry with us. (James 1:5).

Inevitability of taking as given

Though we need to apply our the wisdom of experience in all situations however, there's another rule which is applicable to the present world. This is a flawed world so every interaction can be vulnerable. If we do not wish to feel vulnerable, we should not engage in any kind of relationships. To live the life of perpetual forgiveness, we have to be prepared to suffer the same pain over and time. It is essential to be ready for this. While understanding can reduce the risk however, it will not completely eradicate it completely. In all possible ways it is, the Bible tells us to go to peace.

Be peace-loving with all menand women] and be holy, and without it, no one can have a glimpse of God the Lord (Hebrews 12:14).

Tolerance is a must

Certain characteristics that we see in people within our circle of friendship that we have to be able to accept as individuals. There is no immediate time after an individual has hurt us seven times to abandon them in the name of demonstrating wisdom. It is possible that they have hurt us seven times, and they apologize but we are still required to accept forgiveness and might be vulnerable in certain situations. This is not referring to the most extreme instances. It is important to accept the flaws of those around us, just like the Bible warns us.

If Jesus was the Holy One who lived at heaven and surrounded by a pure atmosphere and holy, could dwell with us, we can't let anyone injured us seven times. Although Jesus was around people who were sinners He was able to bear their iniquities. He suffered the imperfections and mistakes of His Jesus's followers. He was aware of the shortcomings of the people around

Jesus. In the same way, we should recognize this and not be surprised when we are constantly slapped by people. We should, of course, let wisdom protect us however, no amount of wisdom will stop the vulnerability that an imperfect humanity creates in human interactions.

As a conclusion, taking things as a given cannot be denied when it comes to our relationship in this world.

But, we should believe in God to grant us three aspects in our struggle in forgiveness. We can first trust God to assist us in learning to accept forgiveness. In addition, we can rely on God to give us His mercy to accept the flaws, insanity and dissimilarities of people. In addition, we should depend on Him to provide us with insight into how we can manage each situation.

Forgiveness Prayer

Lord, I beg you grant me grace and wisdom to be a good person and forgive despite all odds. I faith in your guidance and wisdom as I walk the path of forgiveness in Jesus the name of Jesus.

We believe he is getting Through This

It is possible that we have valid concerns concerning the reasons why we don't wish to be forgiven. One reason could be the failure to judge that forgiveness is believed to cause. The difficulty is to forgive someone because we believe that the individual is absolved of a offense. But, it isn't the reality. The fact that we are forgiven doesn't mean justice has been inaccessible.

Human experience is a witness to justice. experiences

God is known as the God of Judges on the entire Earth and He administers justice due to His being an equitable God. Yes, mercy is also a factor however it is not in the way of justice. The evidence of His justice in the world. It is as if we "see" an invisible Hand serving justice in odd areas. Even people who aren't religious, specifically people working in the judiciary system, such as judges investigators, prosecutors as well as police officers have witnessed that justice has an ability to be executed. They've seen repeatedly that justice can come from strange sources. This is the act of God, the God in the realm of justice. God is able to punish the wicked and reward the righteous.

However, let the one who glories praise in this know who understands and knows my name, and that I am the LORD that exercise kindness as well as justice, judgement, and love throughout the world and in all these thingsI am content, says God the LORD (Jeremiah 9:24).

God does three or more things in the world of Earth According to this scripture: mercy the act of judgment (the decision-making process in an issue) as well as righteousness (justice). Nobody is able to escape every crime. This is especially true in the time that God is the God of Justice remains in His place on His King's throne. When we accept forgiveness this does not necessarily mean that God has completely forgiven the perpetrator. In no way. If not, then he isn't a just Judge.

The evidence of justice is divine need for inter-personal relationships

The goodness of God can be observed in His importance placed on the way we interact with one another. Jesus For instance, Jesus says that if we take gifts to the altar, and find out that someone is angry with us, perhaps because of how we behaved towards them, we are to put the gift away at the altar. We then have to take the time to sort things out together with the person who is upset. If we do what is right then we are able to return and present the gift to God which He then be able to accept it. It is not possible to go away from one with a heartache and later donate a million dollars at the altar, hoping God will take the gift. That isn't possible. God has intervened. God of justice is at work and in the fight for the person whom we've been unfair to.

Thus, if thou take your offering to the altar and then remember that thy brother has a right to be angry with you and you leave your gift at the altar, then go on your way and first reconcile with your brother and present thy gift (Matthew 5:23-24).

God does have a method to deal with people who harm us because by doing this, they've violated His commandment to be a person of God that is the basis of all Law;

So, whatever you wish men did to you, be sure to do just as to them, as this is the law, and the Prophets (Matthew 7:12).

This is fairness. It is fairness. He is able to see all that we do for our friends and neighbors, and He'll serve justice to the ones worthy of this. No one escapes it.

The thought of this brings me back to what I had promised to do in honor of a brother. He was able to fulfill his own portion of the promise, however I waited to fulfill my own due to the fact that he angered me before. It was nothing to worry about for me as far as it was concerned. A few days later, at the congregation, when I was with him I felt the Lord talked to me, saying that He could see the deep hurt of the man and suggested that I must fulfill my promise to take care of him. I recall being amazed to find out that the Lord took note of the fact that. I lived up to my obligations to the Lord. My God of justice demanded to remove it from my hands.

Leave justice to the care of a righteous Judge

If we are told to forgive, it means that we are giving justice into the God of fairness. God of justice. Naturally, we could be able to appeal to the government or human tribunal, but not. But, generally speaking there is no way to appeal certain matters to an earthly court. For instance, we cannot bring our perpetrator to the court of heaven to complain about our behavior. Our in-laws are not to be blamed as a spouse to court because they have treated us in a way that is unfair. It is our duty to forgiving anyone who has done our wrong regardless of whether or not we received justice from a heavenly government.

Our obligation is to forgive. It is our responsibility to allow them to go. It is no longer our intention to see the offender penalized, as it isn't the case that we are truly accepted forgiveness. Actually in the Bible declares that if you see someone struggling, we must to assist them, and by doing that, God will deal with those who are in need of help very severely. This is an incredibly terrifying thought.

As a conclusion, we should be adamant about not letting go simply because we believe we are forgiving and our perpetrator is getting off with a felony. But not by the length of a sentence. God does the right thing.

Forgiveness Prayer

Lord, let me not be hindered in giving up since I'm getting a slap in the face. I trust that the Judge all over the world is going to do the right thing. Please forgive me for the people who insulted me, in Jesus Christ's name. Amen.

The Person May Think I am Stupid

In the process of letting go the offender could be filled with obstacles. A common roadblock comes in the moment we believe that the person who is committing the crime believes that he's smart, and we're stupid. This can be a source of pain. It could be that he leaked information concerning you, which irreparably hurt your reputation. He may have denied you being promoted, convincing your boss to give your name and select an alternative for the position. Perhaps he has done something that was not right for you, and now you're being asked to be forgiven by God. You may feel foolish. Remember that not letting go of isn't doing something stupid. Why? Let's look at some the possible reasons.

Forgiveness is a suggestion from God, the wise and all-knowing God.

In the event that you are able to forgive your perpetrator while he may think that you're foolish, the fact is you're not. By a far. The most important thing for you is that you're obeying the commands of the sensible God so you can't be foolish. This is the logical conclusion. Be aware of that. Additionally, it is important be aware that the only winning or losing scenario that matters is when you either win or lose in God's court. If you are able to forgive that you have forgiven, you win before God. It is a good motive to believe that you're not in the wrong;. If you're blessed.

He said more so, blessed are people who listen to the word of God and follow the commandments of God (Luke 11:28).

Chapter 15: Keep in mind the importance of the forgiveness of your own

Furthermore, even though it is true that the sacrifice of Jesus is the sole reason for forgiveness by God However, there are other factors that could hinder your acceptance of forgiveness as a Christian. God will forgive you of your mistakes to the extent you also forgive others. If you refuse to forgive, your transgressions are not forgiven. which is a blessing far too valuable to put the value of. If you lose this blessing, it could result in sicknesses, illnesses as well as diseases. This could result in the prayers of your heart being thwarted. It may result in God refusing to show mercy to your life, in the same way that you failed to exhibit mercy on your perpetrator by let him go. Spiritual consequences are for you to imagine.

If you do not forgive the Father who is in heaven, forgive your transgressions (Mark 11:26).

You're obeying God's instruction

In giving up, you are taking a commandment from the Lord. By refusing to let go it is not true that you're admiring His word. It is your choice to be able to forgive, regardless the way people view your situation is the most wise one to take. If you consider God's fear God foolish, consider reconsidering your position.

The terror of the LORD is a wellspring of life that allows us to escape from the death traps (Proverbs 14:27).

Positive effects can have on your mood

Fourth, giving up the offender can bring a wealth of joy to your heart. By letting go of your offender, the anger you feel towards them transforms into the relief of being able to let them go. In addition, when accepting forgiveness, your hurt goes away. The pain you feel after somebody irritates you can be tied to the incident, which means it is when you forgive or release forgiving, the hurt towards the perpetrator also goes away. If someone thinks that this is a mistake you should reconsider. The joy, peace and relief that you feel is worth the price of gold.

The laws of the LORD are righteous to rejoice in your heart. The commandment from the LORD is pure and illuminating your vision (Psalms 19:8).

Positive effects of your lifestyle on health

Fiveth, when you accept forgiveness, you're making your health do a lot of goodness. Negative emotions in the context of being angry release stress hormones that afflict the immune system and can lead to a variety of health risks like heart cancer, heart attacks or high blood pressure the list goes on. If you are able to forgive that you have forgiven, you're not dumb, you're intelligent. The benefits will be felt to be healthy.

A happy heart can be well [like] a remedy But a spirit that is broken hurts in the bone (Proverbs 17:22).

You free yourself from the previous

Sixth, if you are able to forgive the past, you release yourself from the past, and you allow yourself to be open to a new, bright future. This isn't allowing yourself to dwell in the previous past that will create detrimental effects on your relationship with others in the future. The burden of your previous relationship will affect the new ones that God is sending down your way.

The ability to forgive can be a friend, but not being forgiving can be a threat. In forgiveness, you're not foolish and you're being smart. By letting go, it means you have taken the right path: do the opportunity!

Forgiveness Prayer

God, guide me be aware that forgiveness is a sign of with wisdom because I'm taking the counsel of the wise God. My focus should be upon you and your words rather than the words of others and in Jesus Christ's name.

People May Think We Are Weak

The road to forgiveness is filled with hurdles. These obstacles make us reluctant to forgive our perpetrator. One is the impression people think they have. Some people might think that I'm weak-willed or that I am weak-minded as I accept forgiveness. If we hadn't been exposed to those comments from others who have said it, we'd heard the words echoed through our ears every time.

The process of forgiveness isn't being a buckling victim

The reason we could not be willing to forgive someone could be that we believe that we're weak. Some believe we are weak when under pressure, or cannot take on the challenge to prevail; however, this is not the case. The truth is not far off however. Only the strong are able to be forgiven, as they've mastered their emotional states.

www.ingramcontent.com/pod-product-compliance
Lightning Source LLC
Chambersburg PA
CBHW071335120626
46546CB00002B/565